JUNIOR BIOGRAPHIES

Rita Santos

ARIANA GRANDE

POP STAR

Enslow Publishing
101 W. 23rd Street
Suite 240
New York, NY 10011
USA

enslow.com

WORDS TO KNOW

charity A group that helps people in need.

debut First; to appear for the first time.

devastated Feeling great shock or sadness.

empower To give strength and confidence.

encourage To offer support.

karaoke A device that allows people to sing along with recorded music.

maternal Motherly; having to do with mothers.

octave Eight steps in a musical scale.

soprano The highest singing part.

spin-off A show that is based on another show, usually with one or more characters from the original.

vegan A person who does not eat animals or animal products like eggs and dairy.

CONTENTS

Ariana Grande

When Ariana Grande was eight years old, she went on a cruise with her family. One day, she decided to sing karaoke. She got up and sang the popular song "My Heart Will Go On." As she left the stage, a woman asked to speak to her. Ariana was shocked to discover that it was Cuban American singer Gloria Estefan. "This is what you need to be doing," Gloria told her. "You are an amazing singer." Ariana felt encouraged to follow her dreams.

EARLY YEARS

Ariana grew up in Boca Raton, Florida. She loved the beaches in her hometown. Ariana was a good student, but her dark sense of humor set her apart from her friends.

Ariana's voice can hit the whistle register: the highest note human voices can reach.

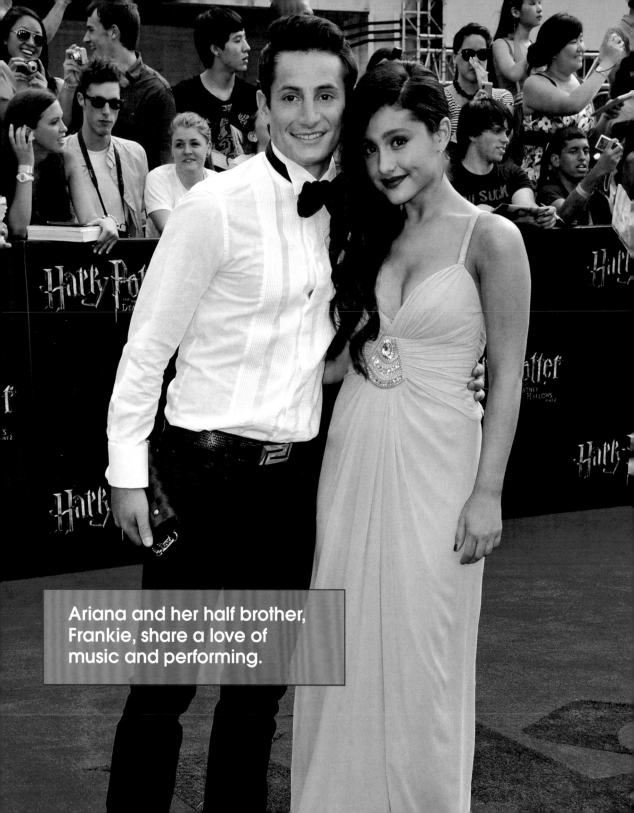

Ariana and her half brother, Frankie, share a love of music and performing.

She tried to make friends with lots of different students to avoid being bullied.

Ariana began working in community theater. Her first role was as the lead in *Annie*. She loved performing. Ariana dreamed of being on the biggest stage of all: Broadway. She was determined to make that dream come true.

When she was performing, Ariana was able to forget about her troubles at home. Her parents divorced when she was eight. She had a difficult relationship with her father, Edward Butera. For a long time they did not speak to each other.

FINDING HER WAY

Ariana was very close to her mother, Joan Grande, and her older half brother, Frankie Grande, who is also a

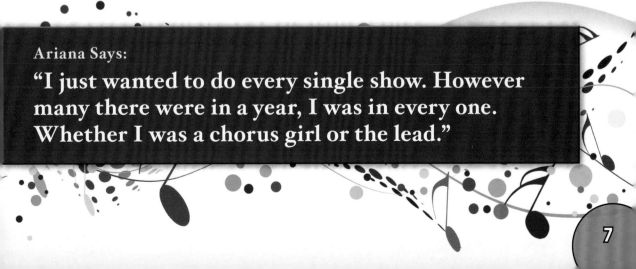

Ariana Says:
"I just wanted to do every single show. However many there were in a year, I was in every one. Whether I was a chorus girl or the lead."

performer. After her parents' divorce, Ariana also became close with her maternal grandparents. They became important influences in her life. They taught Ariana to stand up for what she believes in, even when others disagree.

Ariana was born to sing, and she has a beautiful voice. Singing isn't as easy as it sounds, though. Artists spend years practicing and exercising the muscles in their throat to perfect their skills. In this way Ariana is very gifted. She has a four-octave soprano range.

CHAPTER 2

THIRTEEN AND JUST GETTING STARTED

At age 13, Ariana won the role of Charlotte in the Broadway show titled *13*. The show was about something Ariana knew well— what it is like to be 13! It was the only show in Broadway history to have an all-teen cast and band. Even though her role wasn't large, she won a National Youth Theater Award for her performance. Being on Broadway kept Ariana very busy.

While living in New York City, Ariana sang at the famous Birdland jazz club.

Ariana *(left)* performs with the Broadway cast of *13* in 2008.

She could no longer attend classes at North Broward Preparatory School. Instead, her teachers sent her lessons so she could continue her studies.

THE ROAD TO FAME

Even though Ariana loved acting, she really wanted to be a singer. She had her heart set on releasing an R&B (rhythm and blues) album. But Ariana's manager

Ariana *(far right)* poses with the cast of *Victorious* at the Kids' Choice Awards in 2010.

encouraged her to build an audience as an actress before putting out an album. She knew her manager was right. This led Ariana to take the role of Cat Valentine in the popular Nickelodeon kids' show *Victorious*.

TELEVISION AND MUSIC

Fans loved Cat, Ariana's ditzy but kind character. When the show ended, she was given her own spin-off called *Sam and Cat*. At the 2014

Ariana celebrates with her *Sam and Cat* costar, Jennette McCurdy.

Ariana Says:

"You can be strong and friendly."

Nickelodeon Kids' Choice Awards, *Sam and Cat* won Favorite Show, while Ariana herself was awarded Favorite TV Actress.

Acting wasn't the only thing taking up Ariana's time. While filming television shows, she was also working on her first studio album, *Yours Truly*. It took three years to make the R&B album. Her hard work paid off! Ariana became the fifteenth female artist to have a number one debut album. With her music career finally taking off, Ariana decided to put her acting career on hold.

CHAPTER 3

BECOMING SUPER BUNNY

In 2014, President Barack Obama invited Ariana to sing at the annual White House Easter Egg Roll. She accepted the invitation. Ariana loved singing for young audiences. That same year, she released her second album, *My Everything*. It debuted at number one. At 21 years old, Ariana was on top of the world. She decided she was ready for a more adult style.

A NEW SIDE OF ARIANA

Growing up, Ariana had looked up to artists like Madonna and Lady Gaga, who were well known for both their music and fashion. In 2016, Ariana released her third album, *Dangerous Woman.* She also revealed her fashionable alter ego, Super Bunny. The character wears a black latex

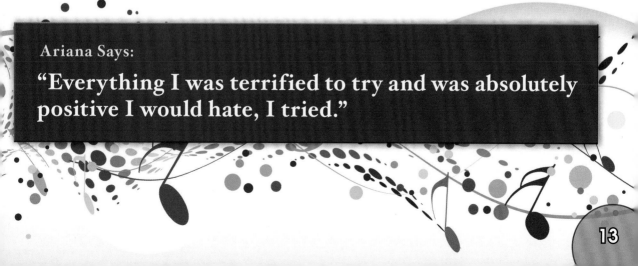

Ariana Says:

"Everything I was terrified to try and was absolutely positive I would hate, I tried."

Ariana performs on *The Today Show* in 2014.

mask with bunny ears and helps Ariana to feel empowered. Ariana was growing up.

Changing the World

As her fame grew, Ariana knew she could use it to raise awareness about issues that mattered to her, like animal rights. Her love of animals made her decide to become a vegan. She does not eat meat or animal products like milk or eggs. This change in her diet is one of the many ways Ariana is trying to change the world for the better.

A concert poster advertises Ariana as her alter ego, Super Bunny.

15

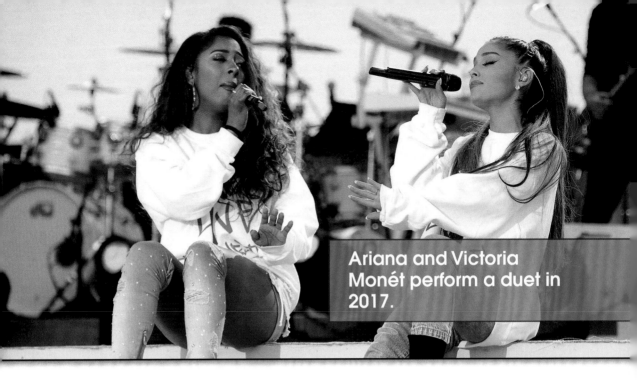

Ariana and Victoria Monét perform a duet in 2017.

Ariana was raised a Catholic but she separated from the church because she disagreed with its treatment of the LGBT (lesbian, gay, bisexual, transgender) community. She shows her support of the community by including LGBT people in her music videos and songs. Also, in 2016, Ariana

Ariana's Super Bunny was a guest character in the video game *Final Fantasy Brave Exvius*.

and singer Victoria Monét released the song "Better Days" to support the Black Lives Matter movement.

Helping others is nothing new for Ariana. She has been doing it since she was ten, when she cofounded the group Kids Who Care. They performed at charity events, raising money for people in need. With all she has done for others, Ariana never imagined that one day it would be her own fans who would need her help.

CHAPTER 4
MAKING A DIFFERENCE

On May 22, 2017, Ariana's Dangerous Woman tour came to the Manchester Arena in England. As fans were leaving the concert, a terrorist set off a bomb in the foyer of the Manchester Arena. Two hundred fifty people were hurt in the explosion, and 23 were killed. Ariana was **devastated**. She stopped her tour to visit with injured fans in the hospital.

HELPING AND HEALING

In June 2017, Ariana organized the One Love Manchester benefit concert to help raise money for the victims and their families. The concert featuring Ariana and several other artists raised $23 million. As thanks for all her support, the Manchester

Ariana Says:

"You learn a lot about love, life, and the people around you during times of crisis."

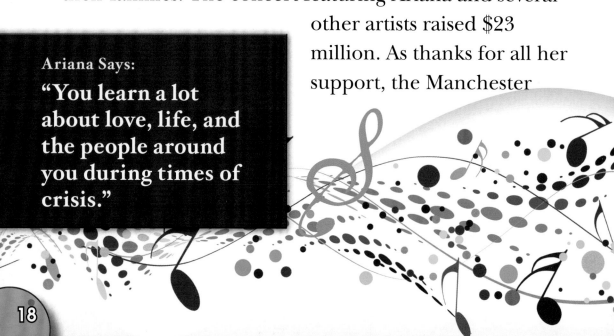

After the terrorist attack in Manchester, people came together to show their support for the town and the victims.

Ariana hosted an emotional concert in Manchester a month after the attack.

City Council named Ariana the first honorary citizen of Manchester.

REACHING FOR THE STARS

Through good times and bad times, Ariana has had the courage, determination, and talent to make all her dreams come true. She never forgets how people encouraged her as a child and how important that was to her. By helping charities like Broadway South Africa, which teaches musical theater and dance to children in need, Ariana is determined to encourage children around the world to reach for their dreams as well.

Ariana dedicated the song "Somewhere Over the Rainbow" to her Manchester fans.

TIMELINE

1993 Ariana Grande-Butera is born on June 26 in Boca Raton, Florida.

2008 Has Broadway debut as Charlotte in the musical *13*.

2010 Lands the role of Cat Valentine on the Nickelodeon show *Victorious*.

2013 *Yours Truly* debuts at number one on the charts. Stars in the spin-off show *Sam and Cat*.

2014 Second album, *My Everything*, debuts at number one.

2016 *Time* magazine names Ariana one of the "100 Most Influential People"

2016 Third album, *Dangerous Woman*, debuts at number two on the charts.

2017 Terrorist sets off a bomb at Ariana's show in Manchester, England, on May 22.
Ariana and other artists perform at the One Love Manchester benefit concert on June 4.

BOOKS

Chown, Xanna Eve. *The New Girl.* New York, NY: Random House, 2013.

Morreale, Marie. *Ariana Grande.* New York, NY: Scholastic, 2014.

Schwartz, Heather E. *Ariana Grande: From Actress to Chart-Topping Singer.* New York, NY: Learner Publications, 2014.

WEBSITES

Ariana Grande

arianagrande.com

Ariana's official website. Provides fans with the latest information on the pop star.

Victorious

nick.com/victorious

Watch episodes of *Victorious* and play games like Cat's Alien Winter Wipeout.

13 the Musical

13themusical.com

Provides information about the musical *13.*

INDEX

Published in 2019 by Enslow Publishing, LLC.
101 W. 23rd Street, Suite 240, New York, NY 10011

Copyright © 2019 by Enslow Publishing, LLC.

Library of Congress Cataloging-in-Publication Data
Names: Santos, Rita, author.
Title: Ariana Grande : pop star / Rita Santos.
Description: New York, NY : Enslow Publishing, 2019. | Series: Junior
 biographies | Includes bibliographical references and index. | Audience: Grades 3 to 6.
Identifiers: LCCN 2017045223| ISBN 9780766097230 (library bound) | ISBN
 9780766097247 (pbk.) | ISBN 9780766097254 (6 pack)
Subjects: LCSH: Grande, Ariana—Juvenile literature. | Singers—United
 States—Biography—Juvenile literature.
Classification: LCC ML3930.G724 S26 2019 | DDC 782.42166092 [B] —dc23
LC record available at https://lccn.loc.gov/2017045223

Printed in the United States of America

To Our Readers: We have done our best to make sure all website addresses in this book were active and appropriate when we went to press. However, the author and the publisher have no control over and assume no liability for the material available on those websites or on any websites they may link to. Any comments or suggestions can be sent by e-mail to customerservice@enslow.com.

Photo Credits: Cover, p. 1 Steve Granitz/WireImage/Getty Images; p. 4 Gregg DeGuire/WireImage/Getty Images; p. 6 D Dipasupil/FilmMagic/Getty Images; p. 9 Walter McBride/Corbis Entertainment/Getty Images; p. 10 Larry Busacca/KCA2010/Getty Images; p. 11 Araya Diaz/Getty Images; p. 14 Kevin Mazur/WireImage/Getty Images; p. 15 Dinendra Haria/Alamy Stock Photo; p. 16 Kevin Mazur/One Love Manchester/Getty Images; p. 19 Ben Stansall/AFP/Getty Images; p. 20 Getty Images; back cover, pp. 2, 3, 22, 23, 24 (curves graphic) Alena Kazlouskaya/Shutterstock.com; interior page bottoms (abstract music notes) Redshinestudio/Shutterstock.com.